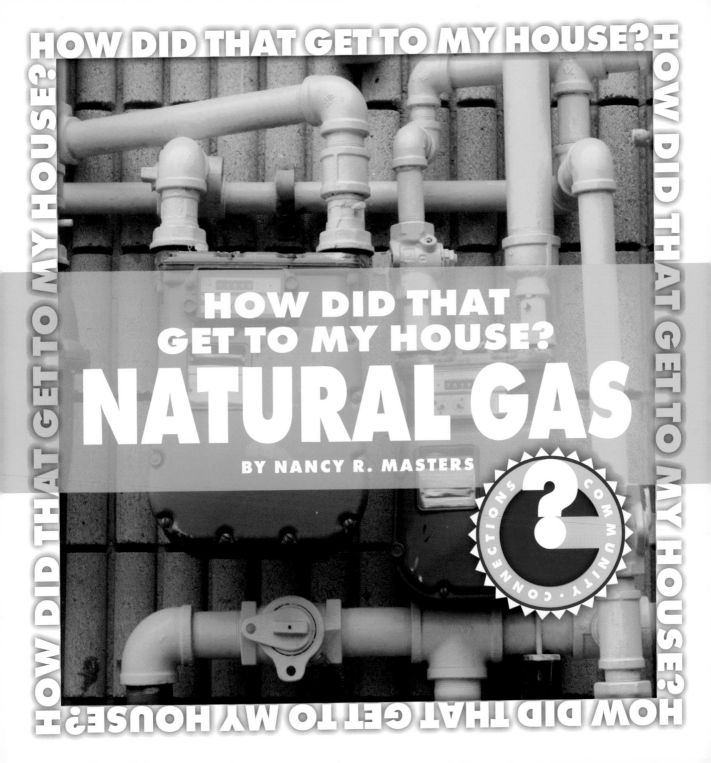

HOW DID THAT GET TO MY HOUSE?
NATURAL GAS

BY NANCY R. MASTERS

COMMUNITY CONNECTIONS

CHERRY LAKE Publishing

Published in the United States of America by Cherry Lake Publishing
Ann Arbor, Michigan
www.cherrylakepublishing.com

Content Adviser: Mary Raber, Associate Director, Institute for Interdisciplinary
Studies, Michigan Technological University
Reading Adviser: Cecilia Minden-Cupp, PhD, Literacy Consultant

Photo Credits: Cover and pages 1 and 9, ©Supertramp/Dreamstime.com; page 5, ©Patsy
Michaud, used under license from Shutterstock, Inc.; page 7, ©Joy M. Prescott, used under
license from Shutterstock, Inc.; pages 11 and 13, ©Devon Energy Corporation; page 15,
©Mark Boulton/Alamy; page 17, ©Nancy Hoyt Belcher/Alamy; page 19, ©J. Waldron, used
under license from Shutterstock, Inc.; page 21, ©oorka, used under license from Shutterstock, Inc.

LIBRARY OF CONGRESS CATALOGING-IN-PUBLICATION DATA

Masters, Nancy Robinson.
  How did that get to my house? Natural gas / by Nancy Robinson Masters.
    p. cm.—(Community connections)
  Includes bibliographical references and index.
  ISBN-13: 978-1-60279-479-5
  ISBN-10: 1-60279-479-0
  1. Natural gas—Juvenile literature. I. Title. II. Title: Natural gas. III. Series.
  TP350.M37 2010
  665.7—dc22   2008053952

Cherry Lake Publishing would like to acknowledge the
work of The Partnership for 21st Century Skills. Please
visit www.21stcenturyskills.org for more information.

NATURAL GAS

CONTENTS

WHAT IS NATURAL GAS?

Click! You see a blue flame on the stove's burner. Hiss! You hear hot water in the dishwasher. Whoosh! You feel warm air blowing from the furnace.

Natural gas is a fuel that made these things happen. Natural gas is a **fossil fuel**, just like oil and coal.

We can use natural gas to cook our food.

We use fossil fuels to make heat and power. Fossil fuels are made from the remains of plants and animals. The plants and animals lived millions of years ago.

Layers of mud and rock covered the plant and animal remains. The weight of the mud and rock squeezed some of the remains. Over time, the remains turned into tiny **methane molecules**.

Methane molecules are trapped underground between layers of rock and mud.

Methane molecules burn very easily. You can't see, taste, or smell them. You can only smell natural gas after a **chemical** is added. The chemical is called **mercaptan**. Mercaptan makes natural gas stink like rotten eggs!

The natural gas inside these pipes smells bad because mercaptan was added to it.

We know that natural gas burns easily. It is important for us to be able to smell natural gas. What might happen if we could not smell it?

9

FINDING AND CLEANING NATURAL GAS

Layers of rock trap natural gas deep under the ground and the oceans. Workers have to dig holes to get to the trapped gas. They use special tools called drilling rigs. Metal pipes are placed in the holes to build gas wells. Gas flows up the pipes.

Workers use tools called drilling rigs to find natural gas.

Natural gas is gathered from gas wells. Then it is sent through pipes to a **gas processing plant**. The gas processing plant cleans the gas. Some clean gas is stored. Some clean gas is sent to cities and towns.

Natural gas is cleaned at processing plants such as this one. Other gases that are mixed with the methane gas are removed.

MOVING NATURAL GAS

A natural gas **transmission pipeline** is like a highway. Gas travels inside the pipes like cars going through a tunnel. **Compressor stations** along the pipeline use valves that work like gates. The valves control the flow of the gas.

Gas pipelines are buried underground.

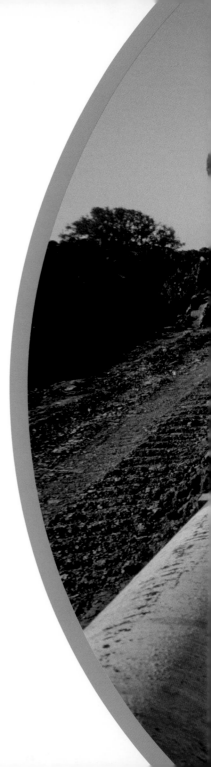

Natural gas pipelines are buried underground. Look for signs near your house that tell where the pipes are buried.

Workers use a special kind of robot called a pig. The pig is used to check for cracks or leaks inside the pipeline. Sending the robot through the pipe is called "pigging the pipeline." This helps natural gas move safely across the country.

Pipelines are built in cities and towns. They take the natural gas from the main pipeline to houses that use natural gas.

Some robots, like this pig, are used to clean pipelines.

Pigs in the Pipeline

Devices called "pigs" improve the flow of oil through the trans Alaska pipeline and monitor its condition. Pigs are launched and retrieved at pump stations and travel through the pipeline with the moving oil. The orange polyurethane sample in this pipe segment is a cleaning and flow improvement pig. Other more sophisticated pigs use magnetic fields and ultrasonic signals to detect small changes in the pipe's wall thickness and shape. Pigs are among the most important tools available for protecting the pipeline and detecting potential problems.

Alyeska pipeline

Each house has a gas meter. It measures how much natural gas goes from the pipeline to the house. Another pipe carries gas from the meter to gas pipes inside the walls of your house. Stoves, water heaters, and furnaces connect to the pipes in the walls.

18

Some big buildings have more than one natural gas meter.

Ask an adult to show you the natural gas meter at your house. Talk about ways you can use less natural gas.

19

Gas scientists are building new tools. They want to drill for natural gas on other planets. Who knows? Maybe someday we will cook on stoves that use natural gas from Mars!

Do you think we could use natural gas from Mars?

GLOSSARY

chemical (KEM-ih-kuhl) a mixture made of molecules

compressor stations (kuhm-PRESS-ur STAY-shuhnz) places along pipelines where valves control the flow of natural gas

fossil fuel (FOSS-uhl FYOOL) fuel made from the remains of plants and animals

gas processing plant (GAS PRAHS-sess-ing PLANT) a place where natural gas is cleaned

mercaptan (mur-KAP-tuhn) a chemical used to give natural gas a smell

methane molecules (METH-ayn MAHL-uh-kyoolz) parts of natural gas you can't see, smell, or taste

transmission pipeline (trans-MISH-uhn PIPE-line) pipes that carry natural gas to cities and towns

FIND OUT MORE

BOOKS

Parker, Steve. *Oil and Gas*. Milwaukee: Gareth Stevens, 2004.

Storad, Conrad J. *Fossil Fuels*. Minneapolis: Lerner Publishing Group, 2008.

WEB SITES

Energy Information Administration: Energy Kid's Page
www.eia.doe.gov/kids
Learn fun facts about natural gas

U.S. Department of Energy—Kids Saving Energy

www.eere.energy.gov/kids/
Links to information, games, and a quiz to help you learn about saving energy

INDEX

ABOUT THE AUTHOR

Nancy Robinson Masters lives in a house that uses natural gas. She likes to read and write in her warm kitchen when it is cold outside.

24